Color Tab Index

ATTRACTING HUMMINGBIRDS

FEEDERS — Choosing, Putting Up, Maintaining

PLANTS — Best Hummingbird Plants, Creating Good Habitat

EASY GUIDE TO HUMMINGBIRD IDENTIFICATION

MALES — Birds with Dark Throats *

FEMALES — Birds with Light Throats *

THE HUMMINGBIRDS   *ARRANGED BY THROAT COLOR OF MALES*

ORANGE	Allen's and Rufous
RED/PINK	Broad-tailed, Calliope, Anna's, and Ruby-throated
PURPLE/VIOLET	Black-chinned, Costa's, White-eared, and Lucifer
GREEN	Magnificent, Buff-bellied, and Berylline
WHITE	Violet-crowned
BLUE	Broad-billed and Blue-throated

* See box on left.

Stokes Field Guides

Stokes Field Guide to Birds: Eastern Region

Stokes Field Guide to Birds: Western Region

Stokes Field Guide to Bird Songs: Eastern Region (CD/cassette)

Stokes Field Guide to Bird Songs: Western Region (CD/cassette)

Stokes Beginner's Guides

Stokes Beginner's Guide to Bats

Stokes Beginner's Guide to Birds: Eastern Region

Stokes Beginner's Guide to Birds: Western Region

Stokes Beginner's Guide to Butterflies

Stokes Beginner's Guide to Dragonflies

Stokes Beginner's Guide to Shorebirds

Stokes Backyard Nature Books

Stokes Bird Feeder Book

Stokes Bird Gardening Book

Stokes Birdhouse Book

Stokes Bluebird Book

Stokes Butterfly Book

Stokes Hummingbird Book

Stokes Oriole Book

Stokes Purple Martin Book

Stokes Wildflower Book: East of the Rockies

Stokes Wildflower Book: From the Rockies West

Stokes Nature Guides

Stokes Guide to Amphibians and Reptiles

Stokes Guide to Animal Tracking and Behavior

Stokes Guide to Bird Behavior, Volume 1

Stokes Guide to Bird Behavior, Volume 2

Stokes Guide to Bird Behavior, Volume 3

Stokes Guide to Enjoying Wildflowers

Stokes Guide to Nature in Winter

Stokes Guide to Observing Insect Lives

Other Stokes Books

The Natural History of Wild Shrubs and Vines

STOKES
Beginner's Guide
to Hummingbirds

Donald and Lillian Stokes

*MAPS BY **Thomas Young***

Little, Brown and Company
New York   Boston

Little, Brown and Company
Hachette Book Group
237 Park Avenue, New York, NY 10017

Visit our Web site at
www.HachetteBookGroup.com

First Edition

Little, Brown and Company is a division of Hachette
Book Group, Inc. The Little, Brown name and logo
are trademarks of Hachette Book Group, Inc.

10   9   8   7

TWP

Printed in Singapore

Library of Congress Cataloging-in-Publication Data

Stokes, Donald W.
    Stokes beginner's guide to hummingbirds /
Donald and Lillian Stokes ; maps by Thomas
Young. — 1st ed.
        p. cm.
    ISBN 978-0-316-81695-3
    1. Hummingbirds — North America —
Identification. 2. Bird attracting — North
America.
    I. Stokes, Lillian Q. II. Title.

    QL696.A558 S77 2002
    598.7'64 — dc21   2001050346

Acknowledgment

We want to thank Bob and Martha Sargent for
reading over the manuscript and giving us many
helpful suggestions. Of course, we take full respon-
sibility for any errors that may have inadvertently
slipped by us during the production of this work.

Contents

How to Use This Guide

This book is divided into three main sections: attracting hummingbirds, identifying hummingbirds, and individual species identification and life history pages.

In the first section we tell you all about attracting hummingbirds to your yard. We start with describing feeders — the different kinds, where to place them, when to put them up and take them down, how to make feeder solution, and how to maintain and clean them. Then we tell you how to transform your yard into a haven for hummingbirds by creating the ideal hummingbird habitat. This is important, for good habitat will eventually help conserve hummingbirds by providing for their total needs.

In the second section we offer you an easy guide to identifying hummingbirds. We start by describing the major differences between males and females, and then further divide these groups by other obvious clues. This will lead you to the name of the bird you have seen. You can then turn to the complete description of the bird in the species identification pages.

In the final section we give complete accounts of the identification and life history of each species that regularly occurs in North America. There are 16 in all, and they are organized into color tabs based roughly on the color of the gorget of the males. We start with complete clues to the identification of the male, then complete clues to the identification of the female. Then we describe the life history of the species, with a range map. The maps have yellow where the bird spends the summer, blue where it lives in winter, and green where it stays all year.

All of this is accompanied by stunning color photographs — the most complete photographic record of hummingbirds ever published. For each species there are 2 or 3 photos of the male and the female, with one picture in which the bird is perched and one in which it is flying. We also usually include a picture of an immature bird and a picture of the nest for that species.

There is also a list of other resources that will help you enjoy hummingbirds, including Web sites, books, and organizations.

Hummingbirds are the magical jewels of the avian world. No matter how many times we see them, we always marvel at their spectacular flying abilities, iridescent feathers, diminutive size, and close association with colorful flowers.

Early European explorers in North America were also amazed at hummingbirds. They had never seen them before because hummingbirds are limited to the Western Hemisphere. There are well over 300 species in North and South America, but only about 16 species regularly enter the United States, some going all the way to Canada and Alaska.

One of the most delightful aspects of hummingbirds is that they are easy to attract. There is a wide variety of

A male Ruby-throated Hummingbird feeding at Indian paintbrush.

feeders and a whole host of flowers, trees, vines, and shrubs that will bring these stunning birds to your yard.

Hummingbirds are closely associated with flowers because a major portion of their diet is nectar. Their other major food is insects — this is where they get their protein. Because of their foods, most hummingbirds are generally only found in North America during the spring and summer months, when flowers are in bloom and insects are active. In fall, these species fly to Central and South America, where they spend the winter.

Many amazing facts surround the capabilities of hummingbirds. They can fly up to 45 miles per hour; their wings beat up to 78 times per second; they eat half their weight in sugar each day; the average hummingbird weighs less than a first-class letter; and even when resting, they take 250 breaths per minute.

There are also many myths associated with these little gems. None of these things is true: they suck nectar (they don't, they lick it up); they mate in midair (no, they mate while perched); they migrate on the backs of Canada Geese (no, they fly on their own).

Even though we have only 16 species of hummingbirds regularly in the United States, they can sometimes be challenging to identify. The males are somewhat easy, because each has a fairly distinctive colorful throat patch, or gorget. But the females and immatures tend to have light throats and often look much alike. There are more subtle clues to their identity, such as the color of their flanks, or whether they have an eyeline, or the shape and length of their bill.

We hope this guide helps you with all aspects of hummingbirds, from attracting them to identifying them to learning about and enjoying their life histories and behavior. We wish you happy hummingbirding!

Attracting Hummingbirds

HUMMINGBIRD FEEDERS

One of the easiest ways to attract hummingbirds is to put up feeders filled with hummingbird solution. Here are the basic things you need to know to have a successful hummingbird feeding program in your yard.

CHOOSING A FEEDER

Types of feeders — There are two types of hummingbird feeders. One is basically a bottle filled with fluid that is turned upside down and drains into a reservoir or a tiny tube. The hummingbird solution is held in the bottle by the vacuum created inside it. The other type of feeder is simply a saucerlike dish with a cover in which there are holes through which the hummingbirds can get to the solution.

There are advantages to both. The bottle-type feeders have the largest capacity; the dish-type feeders are generally easier to clean.

Perches — Some hummingbird feeders have perches and others do not. This is not particularly important to the hummingbirds, since in the wild they often have to hover to get nectar from flowers. However, most hummingbirds do seem to use perches on feeders.

Color — Most hummingbirds are attracted to red because many red flowers are adapted to hummingbirds and their color is a sign to the birds

The upside-down-bottle type of feeder.

The saucerlike-dish type of feeder, with mostly Anna's Hummingbirds.

the hummingbirds. The number of portals determines in part how many birds can feed at once. If you have a lot of hummingbirds coming to your feeders, then you will want more portals per feeder.

A feeder with yellow flower portals being used by a male Magnificent Hummingbird.

that there is abundant nectar within. Having red on a feeder will help attract hummingbirds. Because you have red on the feeder, there is no need for color in the solution, which we do not recommend anyway.

Portals — Portals are the small openings through which humming-birds get to the solution in the feeder. On some feeders they are elaborate and have red or yellow flower shapes; on others they are simply holes. It does not seem to make much difference to

Capacity — Hummingbird feeders come in a wide variety of sizes. Some hold only a few ounces of fluid; others can hold several quarts. The size you use should be determined by the number of hummingbirds you are getting at your feeders and how fast the solution is being eaten. Ideally, you want your solution to be eaten in 3 to 4 days. If it stays out longer, it could turn moldy, especially in hot weather. Because of this, it is best to start out with smaller feeders. If your feeders are drained within a day or two, then try larger ones.

Ease of cleaning — You will need to clean your feeders regularly to be sure that no mold builds up. Therefore, it is important that you can reach all parts of the feeder easily. Check the feeder you buy to be sure that it will be easy to clean.

Mounting — There are three basic ways to mount hummingbird feeders — on a pole, hung from above, and on a window. All are effective; it just depends on your situation. Pole-mounted feeders are good for gardens; hanging feeders from a tree limb or roof overhang is good for keeping raccoons and other mammals away; and window mounts are great when you want to see the birds up close.

An immature male Ruby-throated Hummingbird using a window-mounted feeder.

PUTTING UP FEEDERS

Location — When you are just starting to attract hummingbirds, you want to put the feeders where the birds are most likely to discover them. This means out in the open and preferably near flowers that might also attract hummingbirds. Once hummingbirds have found your feeders you can gradually move them to just where you want them and the birds will follow them. You may also want to put the feeders in a slightly protected area, where they are out of the sun and wind. This will keep the solution fresh longer and keep the wind from swaying the feeders and spilling solution.

Number — Even when just starting out, you may want to try putting out several feeders in different locations, for you never know where the birds might find them. Hummingbirds can be very aggressive in defending feeders from other hummingbirds, so the more feeders you have out, the more hummers you are likely to attract.

Season — Most hummingbirds are migrants and only come to the U.S. and Canada during the warm months. They will show up when and where there are wildflowers in bloom from which they can feed. In the South, arrival may be as early as January or February; in the North, it may be more like April or May. Check the life histories and migration information in the identification pages for the species in your area.

In most of the U.S. and Canada, hummingbirds leave in fall for warmer climates. You will want to keep your feeders up until they are through migrating, for feeders may help fuel them on their journey south. Some people worry that keeping feeders up will prevent hummingbirds from migrating, but this is not true. Hummingbirds are programmed to fly south, most likely in response to decreasing light levels in the shorter days of fall. Males migrate several weeks ahead of females and immatures, even when there is still abundant nectar available from flowers in the wild, so feeders will not keep them from their instinctive journey.

In some warmer regions of the country, such as the West Coast, the Gulf Coast, and the Southwest, there may be hummingbirds that spend the winter due to the availability of nectar from wild and ornamental plantings. In these areas, you can keep your feeders up all year.

MAINTAINING FEEDERS

Filling — When you feed hummingbirds, you should take care to keep fresh solution in the feeders. Filling them with fresh solution every 3 to 4 days is recommended. In very hot climates, you may want to check your solution more often to see that it is clean and clear. If it is cloudy, change it.

Cleaning — Every 3 to 4 days, and more often in hot weather, you should empty your feeders and clean them thoroughly. You can use just hot water or a solution of hot water and a little vinegar to get rid of mold. There are tiny brushes you can buy that help clean the portals and other hard-to-reach parts. Be sure to rinse the feeders thoroughly before filling them with fresh solution.

HUMMINGBIRD FEEDER SOLUTION

The formula — Hummingbird feeder solution is made from water and white table sugar. It is 4 parts water to 1 part sugar (such as 4 cups of water to 1 cup of sugar). Boil the solution for 1 to 2 minutes and then let it cool before putting it in the feeders. If you make extra, you can store it in your refrigerator. It is important not to use anything other than white table sugar, for this most closely resembles what the birds would get normally in flower nectar. Do not use brown sugar, artificial sweeteners, or honey. Some companies sell nectar powder, basically consisting of sugar, to be mixed with water.

Added dye or nutrients — Some commercial mixtures add nutrients or red dye to the solution. Neither of these is

A female White-eared Hummingbird using a perch as she feeds.

necessary. Hummingbirds naturally supplement their diet with insects and sometimes even pollen. And since your feeders are red, there is no need to make the solution red. Additionally, the effect of dye on hummingbirds has not been thoroughly studied.

FEEDER TROUBLESHOOTING

Bees and ants — Bees and ants may be attracted to hummingbird feeders since they also eat nectar from flowers. Ants are the easiest to keep away. Many feeders have little moats, called ant guards, that can be filled with water so ants cannot get across (since they are reluctant to swim). You can also buy a separate ant guard that is hung just above the feeder. This can be used with feeders that do not come with built-in ant guards. There are several ways to discourage bees. One is to buy what are

The yellow bee guard does not stop this male Anna's Hummingbird as he goes for the nectar, but it will keep most bees away from the sugar water solution.

called bee guards and place them over the portals. These are little screenlike covers that keep bees from reaching the sugar solution. Another manufacturer has produced a flexible membrane that fits onto the portals. Hummingbirds can penetrate the membranes, but bees and other insects cannot. Another potential deterrent to bees is to use dish-type feeders and experiment with keeping the sugar water level over half an inch below the portals. Bees and other insects with short mouthparts will not be able to reach the solution. Some people have tried putting a little salad or mineral oil, or Avon Skin-So-Soft around the entrances to the portals. This makes it hard for bees and wasps to get a foothold. Be sure not to get any inside the portals or into the nectar solution.

Raccoons and other mammals — Sometimes raccoons or other mammals will smell the sugar water in your feeders and knock over the feeder pole to get at the solution. In these cases you may need to hang your feeders off a more inaccessible location that they cannot reach. You might try the eaves of a house roof or a high limb of a tree. There are swinging-arm hooks that can be attached to the side of a house, and there are branch hooks available that will enable you to hang the feeder high in a tree.

Hummingbirds chasing one another away — Hummingbirds can be very possessive of a feeder and try to chase all other hummingbirds away. If this is the case in your yard, one solution is to put up several feeders in different parts of your yard or on different sides of your house. This way no hummingbird can defend them all, and you will be able to accommodate more birds.

In general, when there are more than 5 hummingbirds vying for a feeder in any area, they sometimes start to feed at the same time, since no one hummingbird can chase all the others away.

PLANTS FOR HUMMINGBIRDS

The primary food of hummingbirds is nectar from flowers. Hummingbirds take nectar from many types of flowers of a variety of colors, but they often favor long tubular flowers that are red and oriented horizontally. This is because these flowers are specially adapted to hummingbirds and depend on them to be their major pollinators.

These plants have evolved long flowers that only hummingbirds can reach into. The flowers are horizontal, so only hovering hummingbirds can take advantage of them. They are red, which bees and many other insects see as just another dark color, but which hummingbirds see distinctly. Because of all of this, hummingbirds often go first to these red tubular flowers, for they can be assured that there will be nectar and that they will not have to compete with insects. This is why many hummingbird feeders are red.

Therefore, when choosing hummingbird flowers, start with those that are tubular and red. These include a wide range of both wildflowers and ornamental flowers that can be bought at any nursery.

When planting hummingbird flowers, try to create a mass of bloom. Buy several pots of each type of flower and plant them close together. This will help attract the birds to your garden and also supply enough nectar for them to feed on over a long period of time.

Also, try to choose a variety of plants that will provide continuous bloom

This male Ruby-throated Hummingbird is feeding on the nectar from bleeding heart.

This male Ruby-throated Hummingbird cannot resist the red of the hibiscus flower.

Hummingbirds, such as this male White-eared, are most attracted to red tubular flowers.

A male Broad-billed Hummingbird about to feed on the nectar from trumpet flowers.

throughout the hummingbird season. This will encourage the birds to stay in your yard through the warm months.

Here is a list of some of the very best hummingbird plants for each of the major geographical regions of the country. Plant as many as you have room for — from a hummingbird's point of view, you can never have too many hummingbird flowers. (The abbreviation "spp." means that any species within the same genus is also good to use.)

EASTERN AND MIDWESTERN HUMMINGBIRD PLANTS

∽ Flowers

Bee Balm
  Monarda spp.

Blazing Star
  Liatris spp.

Bleeding Heart
  Dicentra spp.

Cardinal Flower
  Lobelia cardinalis

Columbine
  Aquilegia spp.

Coralbells
  Heuchera sanguinea

Foxglove
  Digitalis spp.

Fuchsia
  Fuchsia spp.

Impatiens
  Impatiens spp.

Jewelweed
  Impatiens pallida

Mexican Sunflower
  Tithonia rotundifolia

Phlox
  Phlox spp.

Sage
  Salvia spp.

∽ Trees and Shrubs

Butterfly Bush
  Buddleia spp.

Crab Apple
  Malus spp.

Flowering Quince
  Chaenomeles japonica

Lilac
  Syringa vulgaris

∽ Vines

Morning Glory
  Ipomoea spp.

Scarlet Runner-Bean
  Phaseolus coccineus

Trumpet Creeper
  Campsis radicans

Trumpet Honeysuckle
  Lonicera sempervirens

SOUTHEASTERN HUMMINGBIRD PLANTS

∽ Flowers

Bee Balm
  Monarda spp.

Cardinal Flower
  Lobelia cardinalis

Columbine
  Aquilegia spp.

Impatiens
Impatiens spp.

Jewelweed
Impatiens pallida

Lantana
Lantana spp.

Pentas
Penta spp.

Sage
Salvia spp.

∾ Trees and Shrubs

Bottlebrush
Callistemon spp.

Butterfly Bush
Buddleia spp.

Firebush
Hamelia patens

Flowering Maple
Abutilon spp.

Mimosa
Albizia julibrissin

Shrimp Plant
Justicia brandegeana

∾ Vines

Red Morning Glory
Ipomoea coccinea

Trumpet Creeper
Campsis radicans

Trumpet Honeysuckle
Lonicera sempervirens

WESTERN MOUNTAIN HUMMINGBIRD PLANTS

∾ Flowers

Bee Balm
Monarda spp.

Blazing Star
Liatris spp.

California Fuchsia
Zauschneria spp.

Cardinal Flower
Lobelia cardinalis

Columbine
Aquilegia spp.

Coralbells
Heuchera sanguinea

Crocosmia
Crocosmia spp.

Fireweed
Epilobium angustifolium

Larkspur
Delphinium spp.

Monkey Flower
Mimulus spp.

Paintbrush
Castilleja spp.

Penstemon
Penstemon spp.

Red-hot Poker
Kniphofia uvaria

Sage
Salvia spp.
Scarlet Betony
Stachys coccinea
Scarlet Gilia
Ipomopsis aggregata

∾ Trees and Shrubs
Butterfly Bush
Buddleia spp.
Currant
Ribes spp.

∾ Vines
Trumpet Creeper
Campsis radicans
Trumpet Honeysuckle
Lonicera sempervirens

NORTHWESTERN HUMMINGBIRD PLANTS

∾ Flowers
Bee Balm
Monarda spp.
Blazing Star
Liatris spp.
California Fuchsia
Zauschneria spp.
Cardinal Flower
Lobelia cardinalis
Columbine
Aquilegia spp.
Coralbells
Heuchera sanguinea
Fuchsia
Fuchsia spp.
Impatiens
Impatiens spp.
Indian Paintbrush
Castilleja miniata

Penstemon
Penstemon spp.
Red-hot Poker
Kniphofia uvaria
Sage
Salvia spp.

∾ Trees and Shrubs
Bottlebrush
Callistemon spp.
Butterfly Bush
Buddleia spp.
Currant
Ribes spp.
Madrone
Arbutus menziesii
Manzanita
Arctostaphylos spp.
Salmonberry
Rubus spectabilis
Shrimp Plant
Justicia brandegeana

∾ Vines

Trumpet Creeper
Campis radicans

Trumpet Honeysuckle
Lonicera sempervirens

CALIFORNIA HUMMINGBIRD PLANTS

∾ Flowers

Bee Balm
Monarda spp.

California Fuchsia
Zauschneria spp.

Columbine
Aquilegia spp.

Fuchsia
Fuchsia spp.

Honeysuckle Penstemon
Penstemon cordifolius

Impatiens
Impatiens spp.

Monkey Flower
Mimulus spp.

Pineapple Sage
Salvia elegans

Red-hot Poker
Kniphofia uvaria

Woolly Blue Curls
Trichostema lanatum

∾ Trees and Shrubs

Bottlebrush
Callistemon spp.

Chuparosa
Justicia californica

Currant
Ribes spp.

Eucalyptus
Eucalyptus spp.

Flowering Maple
Abutilon spp.

Manzanita
Arctostaphylos spp.

Mexican Bush Sage
Salvia leucantha

Mimosa
Albizia julibrissin

Mountain Lilac
Ceonothus arboreus

Ocotillo
Fouquieria splendens

Shrimp Plant
Justicia brandegeana

Tree Mallow
Lavatera assurgentiflora

Tree Tobacco
Nicotiana glauca

∾ Vines

Cardinal Climber
Ipomoea multifida

Trumpet Honeysuckle
Lonicera sempervirens

SOUTHWESTERN HUMMINGBIRD PLANTS

❧ Flowers

Aloe
: *Aloe* spp.

California Fuchsia
: *Zauschneria* spp.

Cardinal Flower
: *Lobelia cardinalis*

Columbine
: *Aquilegia* spp.

Indian Paintbrush
: *Castilleja miniata*

Lantana
: *Lantana* spp.

Monkey Flower
: *Mimulus* spp.

Penstemon
: *Penstemon* spp.

Sage
: *Salvia* spp.

Scarlet Gilia
: *Ipomopsis aggregata*

❧ Trees and Shrubs

Bottlebrush
: *Callistemon* spp.

Century Plant
: *Agave* spp.

Chuparosa
: *Justicia californica*

Desert Honeysuckle
: *Anisacanthus thurberi*

Mexican Honeysuckle
: *Justicia spicigera*

Ocotillo
: *Fouquieria splendens*

Shrimp Plant
: *Justicia brandegeana*

Tree Tobacco
: *Nicotiana glauca*

HABITATS FOR HUMMINGBIRDS

In addition to providing flowers and sugar water feeders, there are many ways you can make your yard a more attractive habitat for hummingbirds.

Varied habitats — In general, the more varied habitats you can create in your yard, the more chances you have of meeting the needs of hummingbirds and having them stay longer and possibly even breed. No matter how small or large your yard, you can create open areas with sun, shady areas that are open beneath, gardens with many different types of flowers, a rich variety of shrubs or vines, grassy areas, and even weedy patches. All can be useful to hummingbirds.

Perches — Between feedings, hummingbirds like to perch as they digest their food. They may spend much more time perching than flying, for it only takes them a few seconds to gather nectar from a flower or feeder, but it may take them 10 to 30 minutes

to process it in their system. They do this while perched.

What kinds of perches do hummingbirds like? Some like to perch on bare branches that are about 10 to 20 feet high and at the edge of open areas. This keeps them safe from animals on the ground and gives them a good view of the surrounding area to look for other hummingbirds or any danger they might encounter. To create perches like this, try some medium-sized trees with open branching and not too many leaves.

If you live in a warm climate, hummingbirds will want some protec-

Perches are very important for a good hummingbird habitat. Here a Rufous Hummingbird male rests on a perch between feedings.

tion from the sun during the heat of midday. To help them with this, you may want some taller canopylike trees with places to perch underneath.

If it gets cool in your area at night, hummingbirds may like some dense foliage in which to spend the night and be protected from the cool air and wind.

Some hummingbirds may favor several perches in your yard and return to them time and again when they rest. Some may become territorial around a feeder and choose a perch that overlooks the feeder. From there they can dive down on any intruding hummingbirds and chase them away from the feeder. To handle this situation, see page 15.

By creating a varied habitat with tall trees, medium-sized trees, and a variety of shrubs, you are more likely to also create a place that humming-birds would like to nest. Most of our hummingbirds nest from about 5 to 20 feet off the ground on a horizontal tree limb.

Nesting materials — Be sure to have nesting materials in the area. Some common nesting materials of hummingbirds include mosses, lichens, plant down, bark bits, small

Providing nesting materials and nesting spots in your habitat can encourage hummingbirds like this Black-chinned female to nest.

This Lucifer Hummingbird is perched near a flower where he has a good chance of catching insects, an important part of the diet of hummingbirds.

feathers, pine needles, seed dispersal filaments, fine rootlets, and animal hair. In most cases, hummingbirds use spider silk to hold the nest together. This is gathered from spiderwebs under the eaves of houses, among rock crevices, and any other place spiders build their webs. You may not want to get rid of all of those spiderwebs around the outside of the house: Who knows? Maybe a hummingbird will use them for nest building.

Insects — Hummingbirds do not eat only nectar from flowers or sugar water from feeders. They also eat quite a few insects, which may provide them with the bulk of their protein. If your yard supports a variety of insects, then it will also be good for hummingbirds. If you create a varied habitat with many different levels of vegetation, many different types of plants and flowers, and sunny and shady areas, you will have the best chance to harbor a variety of insects for hummingbirds to eat.

It is essential that you do not use pesticides on any of your plants or on your lawn, for this could injure the hummingbirds you are trying to attract. They may come in contact with the pesticides directly, such as on a flower they are drinking nectar from, or indirectly, by eating an insect that has some of the pesticide in or on it.

Water — Hummingbirds get fluids from flowers and sugar water feeders, so they are not often seen coming to birdbaths for a drink. But they do love to bathe in water, especially if it is misting or sprinkling in the air.

Once, we were watering our garden with a spray nozzle and a Ruby-throated Hummingbird zipped over and hovered next to the water. It then flew through the spray several times, clearly enjoying it, and then flew down to the ground where the water was landing, perched in the spray, and bathed and preened. We were astounded and mesmerized. Then, after a few seconds, it zipped off.

Small fountains with misters or a recirculating fountain that sprays some water into the air can attract hummingbirds. Hummingbirds most often seem to bathe on the wing, flying through mist, spray, or even a lawn sprinkler.

Easy Guide to Hummingbird Identification

When identifying hummingbirds, it is important to know that most adult males and females look different. In general, males have colorful dark feathers on their throats, called gorgets. Female and immature hummingbirds mostly have whitish throats or only small patches of color. This is a good first step in your identification.

When using the key on the next page to identify a hummingbird, first decide if your bird has a dark or light throat, then look at the choices beneath each of these two categories and turn to the section that best fits the bird you have seen. There you will find your hummingbird pictured. If you want more identification clues, life history information, and pictures, you can turn to the main account for that species in the identification pages.

Hummingbirds with Dark Throats

This includes all male hummingbirds except the Violet-crowned male, which has a white throat. It also includes two females with dark throats: the female Buff-bellied and female Berylline Hummingbirds.

Dark throat and dark upper breast

Small hummingbird, red base of bill, go to page 30.
Large hummingbird, all-black bill, go to page 31.

or

Dark throat and whitish upper breast

Rufous upperparts and flanks, go to page 32.
Unusually shaped gorget (throat patch), go to page 33.
Short squared-off gorget (throat patch), go to pages 34–35.

Hummingbirds with Dark Throats and Dark Breasts
Small hummingbird with red at base of bill

Dusky wings, bronze rump
Buff-bellied Hummingbird, page 114

Broad white eyeline
White-eared Hummingbird, page 96

Blue head, turquoise belly
Broad-billed Hummingbird, page 132

Rufous wings, purple rump
Berylline Hummingbird, page 120

Hummingbirds with Dark Throats and Dark Breasts
Large hummingbird with all-black bill

Gray breast
Blue-throated Hummingbird, page 138

Black breast
Magnificent Hummingbird, page 108

Hummingbirds with Dark Throats and Whitish Breasts
Rufous upperparts and flanks

Green on back
Allen's Hummingbird, page 48

Mostly rufous back
Rufous Hummingbird, page 54

Hummingbirds with Dark Throats and Whitish Breasts
Unusually shaped gorget (throat patch)

Streaked gorget
Calliope Hummingbird, page 66

**Gorget corners flare out to
sides, iridescence on crown**
Costa's Hummingbird, page 90

**Long biblike gorget, long
downcurved bill, long tail**
Lucifer Hummingbird, page 102

Hummingbirds with Dark Throats and Whitish Breasts
Short squared-off gorget (throat patch)
Gorget is red

Black behind eye, forked tail
Ruby-throated Hummingbird, page 78

Pale gray behind eye
Broad-tailed Hummingbird, page 60

Hummingbirds with Dark Throats and Whitish Breasts
Short squared-off gorget (throat patch)
Gorget is violet or pink

Violet on lower half of gorget
Black-chinned Hummingbird, page 84

Bright rose-red gorget with rose-red iridescence on head
Anna's Hummingbird, page 72

Hummingbirds with Mostly Light Throats

These include all female and immature hummingbirds except the female Buff-bellied and female Berylline Hummingbirds, which have dark throats. It also includes one male hummingbird with a white throat: the male Violet-crowned Hummingbird.

Conspicuous white eyeline

Small hummingbird, red at base of bill (sometimes inconspicuous), go to page 38.
Large hummingbird, bill always all black, go to page 39.

Buffy flanks

Bill strongly downcurved, go to page 40.
Bill straight, go to pages 40–41.

White or green flanks and no eyeline

Red bill, go to page 42.
Black bill, go to pages 42–43.

Hummingbirds with Light Throats and White Eyelines
Small hummingbird with red at base of bill
(sometimes inconspicuous)

**Short bill, black ear patch, crown black
tinged with bronze**
White-eared Hummingbird, page 96

Long bill, gray ear patch, crown gray and green
Broad-billed Hummingbird, page 132

Hummingbirds with Light Throats and White Eyelines
Large hummingbird, bill always all black

Jagged white line behind eye, tail narrowly tipped with white
Magnificent Hummingbird, page 108

Even white line behind eye, tail broadly tipped with white
Blue-throated Hummingbird, page 138

Hummingbirds with Light Throats and Buffy Flanks
Bill downcurved or bill straight with extensive rufous flanks

Bill strongly downcurved
Lucifer Hummingbird, page 102

Bill straight, rufous flanks, orange-red spots on throat, extensive rufous on base of tail feathers
Rufous Hummingbird, page 54, Allen's Hummingbird, page 48

Hummingbirds with Light Throats and Buffy Flanks

Bill straight, peach flanks, clear throat, limited rufous at base of tail

Long bill, tail extends well beyond folded wings
Broad-tailed Hummingbird, page 60

Short bill, tail shorter than folded wings
Calliope Hummingbird, page 66

Hummingbirds with Light Throats and White or Green Flanks
Red bill or black bill with compact body

Red bill, entirely white underparts
Violet-crowned Hummingbird, page 126

Black bill, bird is compact and stocky

Central iridescent throat spot, underparts scaled with gray and / or green
Anna's Hummingbird, page 72

Clear throat, underparts pale and generally unmarked
Costa's Hummingbird, page 90

Hummingbirds with Light Throats and White or Green Flanks
Black bill and elongated body

Forehead dingy gray, repeatedly pumps tail in flight, long bill
Black-chinned Hummingbird, page 84

Forehead iridescent green, usually holds tail still in flight, medium bill
Ruby-throated Hummingbird, page 78

Resources

Books

Johnsgard, Paul. *The Hummingbirds of North America.* Washington, D.C.: Smithsonian Institution Press, 1983.

Kaufman, Kenn. *Lives of North American Birds.* New York: Houghton Mifflin Company, 1996.

Long, Kim. *Hummingbirds: A Wildlife Handbook.* Boulder, Colorado: Johnson Publishing Company, 1997.

Newfield, Nancy, and Barbara Nielsen. *Hummingbird Gardens: Attracting Nature's Jewels to Your Backyard.* Shelburne, Vermont: Chapters Publishing, Ltd., 1996.

Poole, Alan, and Frank Gill, eds. *Birds of North America.* Philadelphia: Academy of Natural Sciences, 1992–2000.

Pyle, Peter. *Identification Guide to North American Birds, Part I.* Bolinas, California: SlateCreek Press, 1997.

Sayre, Jeff and April. *The Sun Catchers: Hummingbirds.* Minnetonka, Minnesota: NorthWord Press, 1996.

Stokes, Donald and Lillian. *Field Guide to Birds: Eastern Region.* Boston: Little, Brown and Company, 1996.

———. *Field Guide to Birds: Western Region.* Boston: Little, Brown and Company, 1996.

———. *A Guide to Bird Behavior, Volume III.* Boston: Little, Brown and Company, 1989.

———. *Stokes Hummingbird Book.* Boston: Little, Brown and Company, 1989.

Toops, Connie. *Hummingbirds: Jewels in Flight.* Stillwater, Minnesota: Voyageur Press, 1992.

Tyrrell, Esther and Robert. *Hummingbirds: Their Life and Behavior.* New York: Crown Publishers, Inc., 1985.

Williamson, Sheri. *Attracting and Feeding Hummingbirds.* Neptune City, New Jersey: TFH Publications, Inc., 2000.

Yoder, Sylvia. *Desert Hummingbird Gardens.* Paradise Valley, Arizona: Real Estate Consulting and Education, Inc., 1999.

Zimmer, Kevin. *Birding in the American West: A Handbook.* Ithaca, New York: Cornell University Press, 2000.

Organizations and Web Sites

American Bird Conservancy
P.O. Box 249
The Plains, VA 20198
http://www.abcbirds.org

Hummer / Bird Study Group, Inc.
P.O. Box 250
Clay, AL 35048-0250
http://www.hummingbirdsplus.org

The Hummingbird Society
P.O. Box 394
Newark, DE 19715
http://www.hummingbird.org/
hummer.htm

Southeastern Arizona Bird Observatory
P.O. Box 5521
Bisbee, AZ 85603-5521
(520) 432-1388
http://www.sabo.org/index.htm

Photo Credits

The letter following a page number refers to the position of the picture on the page (L=left; R=right; C=center; T=top; B=bottom).

Bowers, Rick and Nora: 24, 26, 33C, 33R, 40L, 55L, 91L, 91R, 93R, 102, 103L, 104, 122, 135R, 141L.

Coleman, Bruce: 16, 30TR, 33L, 40C, 40R, 41L, 51, 55R, 57TR, 61R, 62, 64, 67, 69L, 70, 76, 94, 133R, 134.

Daybreak Imagery: 11, 82.

Holmes, Richard: 140.

Melton, Charles: 13, 14, 39R, 41R, 42C, 42R, 54, 57L, 57BR, 60, 66, 68, 75TL, 78, 84, 86, 87TR, 87BR, 90, 92, 93TL, 99R, 118, 126, 133L, 136, 141R.

Mercieca, Anthony: 7, 18L, 30BL, 30TL, 30TC, 31L, 31R, 32L, 32R, 34L, 34R, 38L, 39L, 42L, 43L, 43R, 48, 49L, 50, 61L, 63R, 69R, 73R, 75R, 79L, 79R, 81L, 87L, 97, 109BR, 111L, 111R, 114, 116, 117, 127, 132, 135L, 139L.

Paonessa, Ralph: 3, 9, 10R, 18, 35L, 38L, 81R, 85, 93BL, 98, 108, 109L, 128, 129, 138.

Rucker, Sid and Shirley: 10L, 17, 30BC, 56, 63L, 75BL, 80, 96, 99L, 103R, 105, 110, 115, 120, 121, 123, 130, 142.

Schlicht, Kurt: 109TR, 139R.

Small, Brian: 25, 49R, 72, 73L, 74.

Smith, Jr., Hugh: 88.

Vezo, Tom: 52.

Identification and
Life History Pages

Allen's Hummingbird

Selasphorus sasin   Length 3.75"

IDENTIFICATION: Adult Male

 Essential Clues

- ✦ Body mostly rufous
- ✦ Iridescent orange-red throat
- ✦ Dull green crown
- ✦ Iridescent green back

A compact hummingbird. Medium-length bill is straight; tail projects well past folded wings. Bright iridescent orange-red throat and white breast. Body is mostly rufous with dull green crown and iridescent green back. **In flight:** Wings make a soft, high-pitched buzz.

These hard-to-see clues help distinguish it from similar male Rufous Hummingbird: Next-to-central tail feathers are not notched, and outermost tail feathers are very thin.

Allen's Male

ID Tips Extensive rufous plumage, as well as green back and green top of head. Tail extends well beyond wing tips.

Allen's Male

ID Tips Extensive rufous plumage and mostly green upperparts. In flight, wings make a high-pitched buzz.

Allen's Male

ID Tips In this view, red iridescence on throat is visible. Note extremely narrow outer tail feathers.

IDENTIFICATION:
Adult female and immature

 Essential Clues

+ *Compact, stocky hummingbird with medium-length straight bill*
+ *Orange-buffy flanks*
+ *Extensive rufous on tail*
+ *May have central spot of iridescent throat feathers*

A stocky hummingbird with straight medium-length bill. Tail is long and rounded and projects well beyond wing tips on perched bird. Throat varies with age and sex from streaked with bronze dots to clear with central spot of orange-red iridescence. Flanks are buffy orange, and upperparts are iridescent green except for rump, which can be tinged with rufous. Extensive rufous on base of outer tail feathers.

Immature male has more heavily streaked throat with blotches of orange-red iridescence,

Allen's Female

ID Tips Note how compact this bird is, as well as orange-buff flanks and clear throat with a few spots in center.

and rufous edging to feathers of upperparts. Immature females have throats streaked with dots, a few of which may be iridescent orange-red.

Although difficult to see in field, next-to-central tail feathers on immatures of both sexes are not notched and outermost tail feathers are very narrow.

Female and immature Allen's Hummingbirds are very similar to female and immature Rufous Hummingbirds, and the two are essentially impossible to tell apart in field. Breeding ranges overlap only slightly, so this can be helpful, and Allen's is less widespread in migration and less often a vagrant.

Voice — Call is very high-pitched, emphatic, buzzy "dzizzt." During chases, call note is followed by lower-pitched stuttering chatter. Not known to sing.

Allen's Female

ID Tips This bird shows orange-buff flanks, rather heavy spotting on throat, and extensive rufous at base of tail.

LIFE HISTORY

Breeding

Breeding range is confined to narrow zone along West Coast characterized by summer fog. Females begin nesting in early to mid-February and usually have second brood. Nonmigratory birds in Los Angeles area may nest almost year-round because eucalyptus, tree tobacco, and ornamental plantings provide nectar all year.

Clutch size: 2; rarely 1, 3, or 4

Incubation period: 12–22 days

Nestling period: 22–25 days

Nest

Nests are placed in dense shaded shrubs or trees. Unlike some other species, Allen's females rarely nest on manmade structures. New nests are often built on top of old ones; this may be done as many as four times on one nest.

Male Displays

Pendulum display — Male does 5 to 10 back-and-forth arcs near an intruder. Near end of each arc, he spreads and

Allen's Female

ID Tips Perched beside nest.

pumps tail, making a rattling noise. Pendulum display may be done alone or may introduce either of next two displays.

Dive display — The male ascends to 50 or more feet at an angle, then does a fast, powerful dive — up to 65 mph —

back to the starting point of display. As he comes to an abrupt stop, his tail makes a buzzing sound. Then he does a brief pendulum display.

Shuttle display — May come before or after pendulum display and may lead to copulation. Male flies forward and backward in tight loops while flaring gorget and creating a rattling noise by spreading and pumping tail.

Other Behavior & Information

Allen's Hummingbirds, especially adult males, are aggressive and territorial, and may chase off much larger birds, such as Red-tailed Hawks. Neither males nor females sing, but both use chip notes as aggressive calls; the male's wings emit a high-pitched trill that serves to advertise territory.

Feeding

Eats flower nectar and small insects, for which it flycatches or probes foliage. The federally endangered western lily is dependent primarily on Allen's Hummingbirds for pollination. Nonmigratory Allen's Hummingbirds are primary pollinators of several "hummingbird flowers" on Channel Islands. Breeding range of migratory birds is almost the same as range of one of their favorite nectar plants, bush monkey flower. At feeders, Allen's Hummingbirds are dominant over slightly larger Anna's Hummingbirds, winning majority of encounters; look for interactions between these two species at your feeders.

Migration

Allen's Hummingbirds begin moving north in December from winter territory in central Mexico and arrive on breeding grounds from January to March. After breeding, they head south as early as May and arrive back on wintering grounds from June to August. The northbound migration path follows coast, while southbound birds fly farther inland and follow mountain ranges, such as Sierra Nevada.

Some Allen's Hummingbirds that live on Channel Islands, off California coast, and in Los Angeles area are year-round residents.

Rufous Male

Rufous Hummingbird

Selasphorus rufus   Length 3.75"

IDENTIFICATION: Adult male

 Essential Clues

+ *Body all rufous; no green on back*
+ *Iridescent orange-red throat*
+ *Crown tinged with rufous*

A stocky hummingbird with medium-length straight bill. Tail projects well past wing tips. Mostly bright rufous upperparts, including rump and uppertail; crown tinged with rufous. A small number have a partially green back.

Orange-red iridescence on throat. Bright rufous face and flanks. Rufous tail with black tips to feathers. Although usually not visible in field, these added clues help distinguish it from similar Allen's Hummingbird: next-to-central tail feathers notched, and outermost tail feathers not narrow. **In flight:** Wings make soft high-pitched buzz.

Rufous Male

ID Tips In this view, throat appears orange-red. Also note black-tipped rufous tail, which extends well beyond wing tips.

Rufous Male

ID Tips This bird clearly shows unique entirely rufous upperparts. In flight, male's wings emit soft high-pitched buzz similar to Allen's.

IDENTIFICATION: Adult female and immature

Essential Clues

+ *Rufous flanks*
+ *Medium-length straight bill*
+ *Extensive rufous on base of tail*
+ *Central spot of orange-red on throat*

A stocky hummingbird with straight medium-length bill. Tail is long and rounded and projects well beyond wing tips on perched bird. Throat varies with age and sex from streaked with bronze dots to clear with central spot of orange-red iridescence. Flanks are buffy orange and upperparts are iridescent green except for rump, which can be tinged with rufous. There is extensive rufous on inner portion of tail feathers.

Immature male has more heavily streaked throat with blotches of orange-red iridescence, and rufous edging to feathers of upperparts. Immature females have throats streaked with dots, a few of which may be iridescent orange-red.

Although difficult to see in field, next-to-central tail feathers on immatures of both sexes are notched and outermost tail feathers are only slightly narrower than central tail feathers.

Rufous Female

ID Tips This bird shows small patch of red iridescence at center of streaked throat. Note orange-buff flanks and extension of orange-based tail beyond wing tips.

ID Tips
This bird's spread tail shows extensive rufous coloration at base. Outermost tail feathers are not noticeably narrower than others. Note also orange-buff flanks and lightly spotted throat.

Rufous Female

ID Tips
Note extensive orange-buff on flanks. Throat is lightly spotted with hint of central iridescent spot.

Rufous Female

Female and immature Rufous Hummingbirds are basically identical to female and immature Allen's Hummingbirds; they are essentially impossible to tell apart in field. Breeding ranges overlap only slightly, so this can be helpful, and Rufous is more widespread in migration and more often a vagrant.

Voice — Call is very high-pitched, emphatic, buzzy "dzizzt." During chases, gives call note followed by lower-pitched stuttering chatter. Not known to sing.

Rufous Immature

ID Tips
Feathers of upperparts have buffy edges, creating a scaly appearance. Throat is quite spotted, and tail shows large amount of rufous.

LIFE HISTORY

Breeding

Usually breeds in second-growth areas, shrub thickets, or forests. Females begin nesting in April, and southernmost breeders may have second brood.

Clutch size: 2

Incubation period: 15–17 days

Nestling period: about 20 days

Nest

Usually placed 1–15 feet high and hidden in low drooped branches of spruce, oak, or other tree. Females may nest in loose colonies. Nest is built of plant fibers and adorned with lichens, bark chips, or mosses. Females may renovate and reuse old nests from past years.

Male Displays

Dive display — Male alternates steep ascents with power dives in either U-shaped or oval pattern. As he passes female, he gives a series of buzzes sounding like a tiny electric saw.

"Whisk-broom" display — Male buzzes back and forth horizontally in figure-8 pattern near female. This display may be done to defend feeding territory from other birds; it has been said to resemble the motion of a whisk broom, hence the name.

Other Behavior & Information

The Rufous Hummingbird is perhaps the most aggressive hummingbird, and it dominates all other similar-sized species.

Feeding

Feeds on a variety of wildflowers, perhaps preferring red tubular blossoms such as those of red columbine. Licks sap from holes drilled by Red-naped Sapsuckers and flycatches for winged insects. Rufous Hummingbirds are fiercely territorial over feeding areas at all times of year, including during migration; they may displace other species, such as Costa's, from their territories.

Migration

In relation to body length, the Rufous Hummingbird has longest migration of any bird in the world. Occurrences in Gulf Coast states in fall and winter are becoming more frequent. As with other hummingbirds, routes are not well-known, but there is evidence that path is elliptical: coastal in spring, inland in fall. Males migrate before females, and immatures migrate last in fall. Earliest spring arrivals on breeding grounds are in about mid-March, although birds do not arrive in Alaska until late April or early May. Southbound departure begins in June. Increasingly, Rufous Hummingbirds are being found east of Mississippi River in fall. Some may come from the North; others may come east from Texas.

Broad-tailed Hummingbird
Selasphorus platycercus   Length 4.0"

IDENTIFICATION: Adult male

 Essential Clues

- ✦ *Rose-red iridescent throat*
- ✦ *Area behind eye pale (rather than black as in male Ruby-throated)*
- ✦ *Long, broad, rounded tail*
- ✦ *Long bill*

A slender long-bodied hummingbird with very long, broad, rounded tail that projects well beyond wings. Bill is relatively long and straight or slightly downcurved. Usually holds body horizontally, unlike more upright posture of other hummingbirds. Rose-red iridescence on throat with pale gray area behind and below eye. Iridescent green upperparts. Flanks washed with light green iridescence. **In flight:** Wings emit metallic trill audible from quite a distance.

Broad-tailed Male

ID Tips Note this bird's long slender shape and pale face. Tail extends considerably beyond wing tips.

Broad-tailed Hummingbird

Broad-tailed Male

ID Tips Note rose-red throat and pale cheek. Very thin outer-most wing feathers create high-pitched buzz in flight. Outer tail feathers show some rufous at base.

Broad-tailed Male

ID Tips Note considerable length and breadth of this bird's tail; it appears almost as wide as wings.

IDENTIFICATION: Adult female and immature

Essential Clues

+ **Long straight bill and long broad tail**
+ **Peachy flanks**
+ **Rufous on tail limited to base of outer tail feathers**
+ **Slender long-bodied bird**

A slender long-bodied hummingbird with long straight bill and very long broad tail that extends well past wing tips. A little like female Calliope that has been stretched. Peachy flanks and pale throat with light spotting or streaking. Upperparts and rump are iridescent green.

Immature male has small patches of rose-red iridescence on lower throat.

Voice — Typical call is high-pitched sibilant chip, "ssssst"; variety of other chip notes may be given. During chases, gives rapid high twitter. Not known to sing.

Broad-tailed Female

ID Tips Note peachy-buff flanks, long straight bill, and extension of tail well past wing tips.

Broad-tailed Female

Broad-tailed Subadult Male

ID Tips This bird shows a very long tail relative to her body size. Outer tail feathers have rufous coloring only at base.

ID Tips This bird has almost acquired complete adult plumage except for small white tips to tail.

LIFE HISTORY

Breeding

At high elevations up to 10,000 feet, in mountain meadows and shrub thickets near woodlands. Females begin nesting in May or June, depending on when wildflowers become available. Especially at high altitudes, one brood is typical.

Clutch size: 2

Incubation period: 16–19 days

Nestling period: 21–26 days

Nest

Usually placed below overhanging branch on horizontal branch of conifer, aspen, willow, or alder at height of 3–15 feet. Nest is built mainly from spiderwebbing and covered with lichens, mosses, and bark. Females may steal nest material from active nests of other hummingbirds and songbirds.

Broad-tailed Female

ID Tips On nest incubating. This may be an old nest that is being reused; note its worn appearance.

Male Displays

Dive display — Male does series of climbs and power dives accompanied by very loud wing noise. He ascends to height of 40–75 feet and then accelerates downward toward female.

"Whisk-broom" display — Male also does display in which he moves back and forth near female in motion like that of whisk broom. He may give chip notes throughout this display.

Feeding

Feeds on flowers with red tubular blossoms as well as many non–"hummingbird flowers" such as pussy willow, larkspur, and locust. Diet includes insects obtained in flight and from foliage. Broad-taileds make use of sap from holes drilled in willow trunks by Red-naped Sapsuckers and are easily attracted to feeders. They are very territorial in defense of feeding areas. Adult males give raspy notes to drive away intruders and frequently are involved with chases; they will even chase thrown rocks. Broad-taileds, however, are subordinate to Rufous Hummingbirds, usually backing down in confrontations with them.

Migration

Routes are unknown, but study has suggested that an elliptical path is used: a more western route in spring and an eastern flyway in fall. Males precede females, which precede immatures in fall. Arrival at southern extreme of breeding range may be as early as late February; northern arrival is in last half of May. Southward migration begins in July.

Calliope Hummingbird
Stellula calliope   Length 3.25"

IDENTIFICATION: Adult male

 Essential Clues

+ *Throat densely streaked with iridescent reddish purple*
+ *Smallest hummingbird*

A small and compact hummingbird with short fairly straight bill. Tail is narrowly notched or square, and short (does not reach wing tips). Throat densely streaked with reddish-purple iridescence; streaks extend outward at corners. White line runs from bill along side of throat. Iridescent bronze-green upperparts. Flanks washed with green and buff.

Calliope Male

ID Tips Note compact stubby appearance of this bird; bill is short and straight, and wings extend just past tip of short tail. Unique streaks on throat appear dark.

Calliope Male

ID Tips In this view, throat streaks show reddish-purple iridescence. Note bird's chunky appearance and short stubby tail with slight notch.

IDENTIFICATION: Adult female and immature

Essential Clues

+ *Stocky and compact, with short bill and short tail*
+ *Peachy flanks*
+ *Little or no rufous on tail*
+ *Smallest hummingbird*
+ *No central spot on throat (but throat usually slightly streaked)*
+ *Tail just shorter than wing tips on perched bird*

A small and compact hummingbird with short, thin, fairly straight bill and short squared tail. Tail does not project past wing tips on perched bird. Our smallest hummingbird. Tail has limited or no rufous at bases of outer feathers. Pale throat may be lightly streaked with dusky spots. Flanks and partial breast band are peachy.

Blotches of reddish-purple iridescence sometimes on throat of immature male.

Voice — Call is soft, high, snapping chip. During chases, gives mix of chatters and buzzes.

Calliope Female

ID Tips Note this bird's compact stubby shape. Throat is lightly spotted, bill is short and straight, and wing tips extend beyond tail. A hint of peachy buff occurs on sides of breast.

Calliope Female

ID Tips Here we see pale wash of peachy buff on sides. Note lightly spotted throat, short straight bill, and short tail.

Calliope Female

ID Tips Notice how stubby this bird's tail looks. Peachy-buff flanks, short bill, and spotted throat can also be seen well.

LIFE HISTORY

Breeding

Breeds at high elevations up to more than 10,000 feet in West, often on mountain slopes. Females begin nesting in May and apparently have only one brood.

Clutch size: 2

Incubation period: 15–16 days

Nestling period: 18–21 days

Nest

Females nest in open mountain forests at heights of 2–70 feet, usually in an evergreen. Nest is often built on top of coniferous cone so that it looks like part of cone, and covered with lichens, mosses, or bark chips. Usually placed under overhanging branch for shelter. Females may reuse nests or build new nest on top of old one.

Calliope Female

ID Tips At nest with two nestlings inside.

Male Displays

Dive display — Male does dive display that is U-shaped. He begins by climbing to height of 30–100 feet, then dives toward female. As he stops dive, faint buzzing sound is made, perhaps by tail.

Hover display — There is also a hover display in which male alternates hovering with short descents starting at about 30 feet above ground.

Other Behavior & Information

This is world's smallest long-distance migrant bird. Despite this, it has not received much attention in terms of field study, so much remains unknown about its life history.

Feeding

Forages for floral nectar, flycatches for insects, and comes to feeders. Also feeds from sap at holes drilled in trees by sapsuckers. Relatively unaggressive, Calliope Hummingbirds appear to be at bottom of dominance hierarchy in hummingbirds. During migration and winter, they may avoid competition with other hummingbirds by feeding on unoccupied less-desirable flowers.

Migration

Calliope Hummingbirds are long-distance migrants; some individuals cover over 5,500 miles annually. Migration route is coastal in spring and inland over mountains in fall. Males migrate a week or so before females and, in fall, immatures migrate a week after adult females. Males arrive in late March at southern portion of breeding range and late April in North. Southbound migration apparently begins in July.

Anna's Hummingbird
Calypte anna Length 4.0"

IDENTIFICATION: Adult male

 Essential Clues

+ *Throat, forehead, and crown iridescent rose red*
+ *Gray breast and belly scaled with green, heaviest on flanks*
+ *Bill short and straight*

A stocky hummingbird with relatively short straight bill. Tail is relatively long and projects past tips of folded wings. Rose-red iridescence all over head, a little like a helmet. Breast and belly are gray scaled with green, heaviest on flanks, and noticeable green tips to the undertail coverts give them a scaly appearance. **In flight:** When hovering, holds tail still and in straight line with body.

Anna's Male

ID Tips This bird is compact and stocky. Note rose-red iridescence on throat and forehead. Underparts are dark and scaled with green.

Anna's Male

ID Tips Characteristic helmetlike rose-red iridescence on head. Underparts dark and scaly, bill short and straight, tail extends past wing tips.

Anna's Male

ID Tips Note very dark and scaly underparts. In this view, iridescence on head looks purplish pink.

IDENTIFICATION: Adult female and immature

Essential Clues

+ *No eye-stripe*
+ *Underparts gray with darker gray or green scaling on flanks and belly*
+ *Patch of rose-red iridescence in center of throat*

A stocky hummingbird with relatively short straight bill. Tail is square and long, projecting past tips of folded wings. Underparts are grayish with gray or green scaling on flanks and belly; upperparts are iridescent green. Adult female has patch of rose-red iridescence in center of throat; immature male has blotches of iridescence on throat and head; immature female has whitish to faintly streaked throat. **In flight:** Holds tail still and straight in line with body.

Voice — Call is a high, lisping chip, "ssip." During chases, gives a hoarse chatter. Song, given by male, is a long string of squeaky, gurgling buzzes.

Anna's Female

ID Tips Characteristic gray underparts with scaled flanks. Note relatively short straight bill and patch of dark feathers in center of throat.

74

Anna's Female

ID Tips Note stocky compact appearance of this bird, gray underparts scaled with green, and iridescent throat patch.

Anna's Immature Male

ID Tips This bird has begun to acquire rosy iridescence on throat and forehead. Underparts are dark and scaly; tail extends well past wing tips.

Anna's Female

ID Tips In this view, red iridescence on throat is visible. Note grayish breast and belly, heavily scaled with green.

75

LIFE HISTORY

Breeding

Anna's Hummingbirds breed in open woodlands and are also common in suburbs in Southwest and along West Coast. Females nest from December to June, earlier than almost any other bird. They typically have 2 broods, and some may have 3. In Arizona, there are a few instances of females laying eggs in October.

Clutch size: 2

Incubation period: 14–19 days (average 16)

Nestling period: 18–26 days (average about 20)

Nest

An Anna's Hummingbird nest is a typical hummingbird nest, bound together with spider silk and coated with lichens, and is most often placed on horizontal branch 6–15 feet above ground. Females may use paint chips as substitute for lichens. Nests are not reused and new nests are seldom built on top of old ones; however, material from old nests is employed in building new nest.

Anna's Female

ID Tips On nest incubating.

Male Displays

Dive display — This display lasts about 12 seconds and begins with male singing and hovering 6 feet or more above female. He then ascends 70–130 feet and dives almost straight down, stopping within a yard of female, where he gives a loud squeak. He then flies back to where he began display.

"Chatter-sway" display — This display is given by territorial males to drive intruders out of territory. Male sits facing intruder, spreads tail, and chatters loudly while swaying from side to side. A chase often follows.

Shuttle display — Male flies in side-to-side arcs inches above female while uttering buzzy notes. This display may lead to mating.

Other Behavior & Information

Anna's Hummingbird's song is quite complex, and individuals must learn it through imitation. Males may sing at any time of year if defending feeding territory. Male fledglings may attempt singing and dive displays to establish territories. Anna's Hummingbirds will dive at much larger birds, including Cooper's Hawks and Red-tailed Hawks.

Feeding

Catches insects in flight or takes them from crevices, stream banks, and spiderwebs. Anna's Hummingbirds tend to be dominated by Allen's Hummingbirds, the other West Coast breeder; in West, you can observe these two species interacting at feeders.

Migration

Anna's Hummingbird is a very short-distance migrant, perhaps best described as nomadic — just moving on to nearest productive feeding area when needed. Movement back to breeding grounds begins in late October to early November in Arizona and New Mexico. After nesting season, males leave territories in late June or early July, with females and immatures leaving later. Birds go in all directions except due west — some head southeast as far as New Mexico or Mexico; others go north along coast of British Columbia.

Ruby-throated Hummingbird

Archilochus colubris Length 3.75"

Ruby-throated Male

ID Tips Note ruby-red iridescence on throat and unique black patch that runs from bill to behind eye.

IDENTIFICATION: Adult male

 Essential Clues

+ *Most widespread hummingbird in East*
+ *Iridescent ruby-red throat*
+ *Black patch extends from below bill to behind and below eye*
+ *Tail strongly notched*

Most widespread hummingbird in North America and most common species that breeds in East. A small slender hummingbird whose body tapers to thin neck. Bill is medium length and straight. Tail is strongly notched and projects noticeably beyond wing tips. Throat is bright iridescent crimson. Black patch extends from below bill to behind and below eye. Bright golden-green upperparts; whitish underparts. Flanks washed with greenish or greenish buff. Bright iridescent green crown and forehead. **In flight:** Tail is held still while hovering. Wings produce soft high-pitched buzz audible at close range.

Ruby-throated Male

ID Tips In this view head looks all dark. Note straight bill, white collar, emerald-green upperparts, and strongly notched tail.

Ruby-throated Male

ID Tips Note short squared-off gorget and green iridescence on flanks.

IDENTIFICATION: Adult female and immature

Essential Clues

+ *No eye-stripe*
+ *Elongated body*
+ *Greenish flanks*
+ *Emerald-green forehead and upperparts*
+ *Holds tail still in flight (does not constantly flip it)*

Most widespread hummingbird in North America and most common species in East. A small elongated hummingbird with medium-length straight bill. Tail is relatively long, projecting noticeably beyond wing tips when bird is perched. Underparts are white; throat can have dusky spots; flanks can be green. Upperparts, including forehead, are bright green (unlike Black-chinned female, which has grayish-brown forehead but is otherwise very similar). Tail held still in flight.

Immature males often have some iridescent red spots on throat.

Voice — Call is high squeaky "dit" or "didit." During chases, gives squeaky three-part chatter, "dzzt, chikididit-chidit." Song, given by the male, is a series of soft high-pitched "tee" notes.

Ruby-throated Female

ID Tips Note hint of green coloration on forehead. Underparts are whitish with dingy greenish-gray flanks; throat has dusky spots. Tail extends noticeably beyond wing tips.

Ruby-throated Female

ID Tips Note brilliant emerald-green upperparts, including forehead, and clean white underparts with grayish flanks. Bill is medium length and straight.

Ruby-throated Immature

ID Tips This bird's forehead is noticeably green. Pale buffy edges to crown feathers give it a scaly appearance characteristic of immatures. Note hint of black mask.

LIFE HISTORY

Breeding

Breeds in several habitats, such as forests, edges of clearings, gardens, and orchards. Females begin nesting in March at southern portion of their breeding range and in May at northern end. They often have second brood and sometimes third.

Clutch size: 2; occasionally 1, seldom 3

Incubation period: 12–14 days

Nestling period: 18–22 days

Nest

Placed in either conifer or deciduous tree, usually near tip of branch that hangs down. Nest height is 6–50 feet. It is built mainly with fluff from plants such as dandelions and thistle, held together with spider silk and coated with lichens. Females may make improvements to old nests and reuse them.

Male Displays

Dive display — Male alternates short ascents and dives in U-shaped pattern 10–40 feet in height.

Ruby-throated

ID Tips Two nestlings sitting in nest. Note lichens adorning exterior of nest.

Shuttle display — Male flies back and forth in horizontal arcs centered around female, all the while spreading his tail. She may move her head to follow his movements. Females also sometimes do shuttle displays.

Other Behavior & Information

Ruby-throated Hummingbirds are aggressive in territorial defense and will jab at intruders with their bills or swat them with their feet. Fledglings may be almost 1.5 times heavier than adults. Predators include dragonflies, praying mantises, frogs, and snakes. Spiderwebs can also trap hummingbirds.

Feeding

Readily attracted to hummingbird feeders. Ruby-throated Hummingbirds show a preference for flowers with red tubular blossoms. They also catch insects in flight or by picking them off bark or taking them from spiderwebs. They visit sap "wells" — holes drilled by Yellow-bellied Sapsuckers — to drink sap and eat insects attracted to sap. This species pollinates many different flowers; in particular, trumpet creeper is adapted to pollination by Ruby-throats. Subordinate to Rufous Hummingbirds, which occur in small numbers along Gulf Coast in late summer.

Migration

Ruby-throated Hummingbirds winter mainly in southern Mexico. In spring, they arrive along Gulf Coast of United States as early as late February and reach northern part of breeding range in first half of May. In fall, southbound migration begins in early July or early August. As with other hummingbirds, males usually migrate before females, and immatures migrate south after females. In both directions, many birds fly across Gulf of Mexico, while others follow Texas Gulf Coast. Early northbound migrants may rely on sap wells from sapsuckers for energy. Southbound migrants seem to follow blooming of jewelweed.

Black-chinned Hummingbird

Archilochus alexandri   Length 3.75"

IDENTIFICATION: Adult male

Essential Clues

+ *Throat black on upper half, deep iridescent purple on lower half*
+ *White "collar" wraps around onto side of neck*
+ *Long slightly downcurved bill*

A small and slender hummingbird whose body tapers to thin neck. Bill long and downcurved (the longest bill of small hummingbirds). Throat mostly black with deep purple iridescence on lower half; entire head may look black in certain light. White "collar" wraps onto back of neck. Tail extends only slightly beyond tips of long wings. Dull bronze-green or gray-green upperparts, dingy grayish-white underparts. Flanks dull bronze to grayish-green. **In flight:** Pumps tail up and down constantly in flight. Tail has shallow or no notch. Wings emit metallic whirring "zizzz."

Black-chinned Male

ID Tips Note white collar, dark throat, and long slightly downcurved bill. Flanks are iridescent green, and tail extends past wing tips.

Black-chinned Male

ID Tips Note distinctive iridescent purple lower half of throat.

IDENTIFICATION: Adult female and immature

Essential Clues

+ *No eye-stripe*
+ *Elongated body*
+ *Flanks washed with grayish green to dull bronze*
+ *Long slightly downcurved bill*
+ *Forehead gray*
+ *Constantly pumps tail in flight*

This is a small elongated hummingbird. Bill is long and slightly downcurved. Upperparts dull bronze-green or gray-green; underparts whitish. Flanks washed with dull bronze- to grayish green. Throat is whitish, sometimes marked with dusky spots or streaks. Forehead dull gray. Tail extends just beyond tips of long wings. **In flight:** Flips tail up and down constantly while flying; this is an excellent clue.

Immature males often have some iridescent purple spots on lower throat.

Voice — Call is high-pitched "tsip" or "tidip." During chases, gives chattering "zeet dz-z-z-zit." Song, rarely given and done by male, is faint high-pitched warble.

Black-chinned Female

ID Tips Note slim elongated body of this bird. Bill is relatively long and downcurved; tail extends beyond wing tips.

Black-chinned Hummingbird

Black-chinned Female

ID Tips This bird appears quite slender. Note that flanks are washed with grayish and have a few flecks of green iridescence.

Black-chinned Female

ID Tips This bird shows distinctive gray forehead. Note also rather dull grayish-green color of upperparts.

Black-chinned Immature Male

ID Tips Grayish-buff edgings to crown feathers, characteristic of many immature hummingbirds, make him appear scaly. Note small splotches of color on throat.

LIFE HISTORY

Breeding

Black-chinned Hummingbirds occupy a wide variety of habitats, from deserts to cities. Females begin nesting in mid-March at some southwestern locations and as early as mid-April elsewhere. A second brood in midsummer is typical and may be started while female is still feeding young from first brood.

Clutch size: 2; occasionally 3

Incubation period: 12–16 days

Nestling period: about 21 days

Nest

Nests are placed in a wide variety of trees, vines, and other plants; favored locations are in canyons and near water. Nest is made out of downy plant fibers taken from willows or undersides of sycamore leaves, bound with spiderwebs, and coated with lichens only when this helps camouflage it — otherwise lichens are not usually used. New nests are sometimes built on top of old ones. Egg-laying starts before nest is complete.

Black-chinned Female

ID Tips At nest feeding nestlings. Note lack of lichens on outside of nest, which is anchored to leaf with spiderwebbing.

Male Displays

Dive display — Male does series of about 5 to 10 dives in J-shaped pattern, usually in presence of female. This display is presumed to be part of courtship but may also be done to other birds. At bottom of each dive, short tinkling notes are given.

Shuttle display — This consists of a series of back-and-forth lateral arcs or loops, performed by male in front of, and quite close to, female. His wings emit droning sound throughout.

Other Behavior & Information

In territorial fights, Black-chinned Hummingbirds face each other with bills almost touching; each tries to hover above the other and use its bill, wings, or claws as weapons. Such fights rarely lead to injury.

Feeding

Like other hummingbirds, the Black-chinned eats flower nectar, sugar water from feeders, and spiders. It flycatches, probes foliage, or raids spiderwebs for small insects. Black-chinned Hummingbirds are usually subordinate to

Violet-crowned, Blue-throated, Rufous, Broad-billed, Anna's, and Broad-tailed Hummingbirds; they tend to dominate Costa's Hummingbirds and almost always dominate Lucifer Hummingbirds. Female Black-chinneds sometimes chase males away from feeding areas. Watch for these interactions at wildflowers and feeders.

Migration

Males arrive in southernmost part of breeding range in mid-March to early April; in north, they generally arrive in early to mid-May. Males migrate a week or two before females. Adult males begin to leave breeding grounds in mid- to late June in north, mid-July in south; females and immatures leave later. Wintering grounds are in west-central Mexico, but this has not been well studied.

Costa's Hummingbird
Calypte costae Length 3.5"

IDENTIFICATION: Adult male

 Essential Clues

+ *Purple iridescent throat and crown*
+ *Throat has elongated "whiskers" at lower corners*

A small and rather stout-looking humming-bird with short rounded tail and short slightly downcurved bill. Wings extend to or beyond tail. Purple iridescent throat and crown; colored throat has long thin "whiskers" at lower corners. White line over eye and white patch on side of neck. Iridescent grayish-green upperparts; underparts grayish white with some green iridescence on flanks.

Costa's Male

ID Tips Note dark throat's elongated corners, showing some purple iridescence. This bird is very compact, with downcurved bill and wing tips extending beyond stubby tail.

Costa's Male

ID Tips This bird has a "helmeted" appearance, with purple iridescence on throat and forehead. Note long "whiskers" at corners of throat.

Costa's Male

ID Tips Note bright white patch on side of head, long purple "whisker," and compact stubby shape. Flanks are extensively mottled with iridescent green.

IDENTIFICATION: Adult female and immature

 Essential Clues

+ *Compact and short tailed*
+ *No eye-stripe*
+ *Underparts pale and generally unmarked; sometimes greenish tinge to flanks*
+ *Bill short, downcurved*
+ *Faint gray cheek patch*

A compact bird that appears pot-bellied. It has short bill and short tail that just reaches tips of folded wings. Throat is pale and generally unmarked; underparts are whitish, sometimes with greenish wash on flanks. It has pale gray cheek patch. A few adult females develop partial violet gorget.

Immature male has blotches of purple iridescence on throat and head.

Voice — Call is simple "tsit," like call of Northern Cardinal. During chases, gives a variety of chatters, call notes, and squeaks. Song, given by male, is distinctive shrill whine, "wheee-oooo," with first part ascending and second part sharply descending.

Costa's Female

ID Tips Note compact pot-bellied shape of this bird. Bill is slightly downcurved, and there is a blurry gray cheek patch. Wing tips just reach tip of tail.

Costa's Female

ID Tips: One of the occasional females with a patch of iridescence on throat. Bill is somewhat downcurved, and wing tips extend just to tip of tail.

Costa's Female

ID Tips: This bird is compact and stout. Note short stubby tail, gray cheek patch, and plain grayish-white underparts.

Costa's Immature Male

ID Tips: This bird shows blotches of purple iridescence on throat and head. Wing tips reach just barely past tip of tail.

93

LIFE HISTORY

Breeding

Costa's Hummingbirds breed in dry desert scrub. In the southwestern corner of U.S. breeding range, females begin nesting in February or March, and in April elsewhere.

Clutch size: 2

Incubation period: 15–18 days

Nestling period: 20–23 days

Nest

Nest is usually placed within 6 feet of ground in shrub or small tree. Perhaps due to hot climate, nest is loosely assembled, shallow, and flimsy. It is built with feathers and plant matter bound together with spiderwebbing. Females may build new nest on top of old one. Loose colonies of nests have been observed.

Costa's Female

ID Tips On nest incubating. Note somewhat loose construction of nest.

Male Displays

Loop display — Male does a series of loops in vertical plane. He starts by flying around female, then climbs to height of about 75 feet or more. During downward part of each loop, he gives a short whistle. Loops are an elongated oval; entire display consists of 6–40 loops in all. After completing last loop, male flies away from female in a zig-zag path.

Mating display — In courtship, male also does a series of short flights at female. This brief display is believed to initiate mating.

Other Behavior & Information

Its preference for hot dry habitats makes this species unique among North American hummingbirds. Sensitive to predation by Greater Roadrunners and Curve-billed Thrashers, Costa's Hummingbirds will avoid feeding when either of these two birds is present. Females nesting near one another may band together to mob shrikes, jays, wrens, and ravens.

Feeding

Favors nectar from ocotillo, chuparosa, penstemon, and sage. Occasionally visits feeders, but much less frequently than Anna's Hummingbird, to which it is subordinate. Like other hummingbirds, flycatches for insects and takes them from plants. Costa's Hummingbirds are basically subordinate to most other species that they typically encounter.

Migration

Costa's Hummingbird migration schedules vary across breeding range. In southwesternmost part of range, they arrive in February; at northern extreme they arrive in May. Earliest adult males begin to migrate away from breeding grounds in May, a month before females and immatures. Northern birds, however, depart in July. Main winter range is in northwestern Mexico, but some birds overwinter in extreme southern California. The Costa's Hummingbird also occurs as a vagrant along Northwest coast as far as Alaska.

White-eared Hummingbird
Hylocharis leucotis   Length 3.75"

IDENTIFICATION: Adult male

Essential Clues

+ *Red bill (black tip)*
+ *Dark throat and breast*
+ *Broad white stripe behind eye*

A small rather stocky hummingbird with steep forehead and high rounded crown. Short straight bill is red with distinct black tip. Chin and forehead are iridescent bluish purple; breast and belly are iridescent green with white streak down center of belly. A broad white stripe starts at and continues past eye to side of the neck. Upperparts are green with rump feathers edged with bronze.

White-eared Male

ID Tips Notice white line behind eye, red-based bill, dark blue forehead and upper throat, and green lower throat. Rump feathers have buffy edges.

White-eared Male

ID Tips This view shows broad, bright white line behind eye. Also note red bill, green-scaled underparts, and distinctive high rounded crown.

IDENTIFICATION: Adult female and immature

Essential Clues

+ *Broad white line over and behind eye*
+ *Black ear patch and dark crown*
+ *Small*
+ *Red at base of bill or just at base of lower mandible*

A small hummingbird with broad white stripe that runs from above eye to side of neck. It has short straight bill, noticeably steep forehead, and high rounded crown. It has black ear patch, and crown feathers are blackish with bronze edges. Bill is red at base or red just at base of lower mandible. Throat, breast, and flanks are dull white and heavily marked with green spots. Back and rump feathers are dark green.

Immature males have some purplish iridescence on chin; juvenile's bill is reddish only at base, otherwise blackish. Outer tail feathers of immatures have whitish tips; those of adult females have grayish tips.

White-eared Female

ID Tips Note broad, bright white line behind eye, high rounded crown, red base of bill, and black ear patch. Underparts are spotted with iridescent green.

Voice — Call is high-pitched toneless "kit," often strung together and sounding like skittering call of Chimney Swift. Song, given by male, is a series of doubled chip notes, "ki-dit, ki-dit, ki-dit."

White-eared Female

ID Tips In this view, note white eyeline, black ear patch, and heavy green spotting on underparts.

White-eared Immature Male

ID Tips Dark iridescence on throat shows this is a male. Upperpart feathers have buffy edges typical of immatures. Also note red base to bill and green-spotted underparts.

LIFE HISTORY

Breeding

White-eared Hummingbirds breed in mountain forests at high elevations, mainly in undergrowth of pine and oak forests. There are only a few records of nesting in Arizona. Females begin nesting in May; there are no known records of a second brood in U.S., though this is probably common in Mexico.

Clutch size: 2

Incubation period: 14–16 days

Nestling period: about 23–26 days

Nest

Usually placed in shrubs or short trees, especially oaks, from 5–30 feet above ground. Nest is built with downy material from undersides of oak leaves, as well as other plant material, bound with spiderwebbing, and coated with lichens or mosses. Females may reuse nests or build new nest on top of old one.

Male Displays

In "lek" system, up to 7 males gather on singing grounds spaced about 40 feet apart from one another on exposed perches. As they utter low-pitched bell-like notes, a female may approach and lure one male to her nesting area. This male then performs looping flights all around female as she perches, and at times the two of them hover face-to-face. They then fly together in looping maneuvers before going off to mate.

Feeding

The White-eared Hummingbird visits a wide variety of flower species of many shapes and sizes, though it favors mints and penstemon. Like other hummingbirds, it flycatches for insects and takes them off flowers. When foraging on penstemon, White-eared Hummingbirds use a low flight path in order to avoid detection by Blue-throated and Magnificent Hummingbirds, which dominate and drive them away. However, this species is aggressive and often chases larger hummingbirds from feeders.

Migration

Most of population are year-round residents in Mexico, but some White-eared Hummingbirds are present in southernmost Arizona each summer. Dates of occurrence span from April to September.

Lucifer Hummingbird
Calothorax lucifer   Length 3.5"

IDENTIFICATION: Adult male

 Essential Clues

+ *Extensive rosy-purple throat patch with scalloped lower edge*
+ *Long downcurved bill*
+ *Pointed tail projects way beyond folded wings*

This species appears elongated due to long bill and tail. Bill is also strongly downcurved, and tail projects way past folded wings. Throat patch is rosy purple and noticeably long and broad, with scalloped lower edge slightly longer at corners. Crown is dull green; rest of upperparts are iridescent green. Flanks are dark green and breast is white. **In flight:** Note deeply forked tail.

Lucifer Male

ID Tips Note characteristic long downcurved bill and very long pointed tail. Purplish throat patch is long and relatively narrow.

Lucifer Male

ID Tips This bird appears slender and very elongated due to long bill and tail. Note purple iridescence on throat.

Lucifer Male

ID Tips Purple iridescence on throat shows well in this view. Note also long deeply forked tail.

IDENTIFICATION: Adult female and immature

Essential Clues

+ *Buffy flanks and breast band*
+ *Long downcurved bill*
+ *Black line between eye and base of bill*
+ *Gray cheek patch*
+ *Long tail*

This small hummingbird has very long downcurved bill, buffy flanks, and buffy breast band. Tail is long, rounded, and extends well past wing tips on perched bird. Throat is plain and whitish to pale buff. Outer tail feathers are rufous at base, and tail has white spots at corners. There is a black line from eye to base of bill, and gray cheek patch.

Immature male has spots of rose-purple iridescence on throat.

Voice — Call is an abrupt squeaky "kip," sometimes doubled or tripled. Also gives louder more musical chip in series. "Song," given by male, is faint squeaky buzzes.

Lucifer Female

ID Tips This bird's very long downcurved bill is unique. Also note buffy flanks, thick black line from bill to eye, unmarked throat, and gray cheek patch.

Lucifer Female

LIFE HISTORY

Breeding

The Lucifer Hummingbird breeds on sloping dry, scrubby, open areas at elevations between 3,500 and about 5,000 feet. Timing varies according to availability of nectar. When it is plentiful, females begin nesting in April and have a second brood. In years of nectar scarcity, they may wait until June to breed.

Clutch size: 2

Incubation period: about 15 days

Nestling period: 19–24 days

Nest

Nest is placed in cactus or shrub at height of 2–10 feet. It is built with a variety of materials — plant fibers, seeds, twigs, feathers, flower heads — held together with spiderwebbing and coated with tiny leaves for camouflage. Previous year's nest may be used as foundation for new nest, but in years of 2 broods, second involves new nest in different plant. Females sometimes steal material from one another's nests.

Male Displays

Shuttle and dive display — Male Lucifers may display to females at nest, mostly during construction or egg laying. Display is series of side-to-side shuttle flights followed by 60-foot-or-more vertical ascent and rapid dive almost straight down at nest. Male stops dive beside nest and then darts erratically away. During shuttle flights, his tail waves up and down while a loud noise like cards being shuffled is made. Males also do shorter series of shuttle flights to nestlings or eggs in nest.

Other Behavior & Information

Population in Big Bend area of Texas is roughly 50 pairs of adults. Females defend nest site from potential predators like Scott's Orioles and Loggerhead Shrikes.

Feeding

Feeds on various flowers; supplements diet with flies and spiders and comes to feeders. Lucifer Hummingbirds in Texas feed on nectar-rich agaves, although they do not pollinate them. Lucifers are subordinate to Black-chinned

Hummingbirds and prefer to visit unoccupied agaves to avoid contact with them.

Migration

Little is known about migration of Lucifer Hummingbirds; limits of their breeding and winter ranges are unknown as well. U.S. population is known to be migratory, however. Birds arrive in Texas in late March and leave in September; in Arizona and New Mexico, dates of occurrence are from April to September.

Magnificent Hummingbird
Eugenes fulgens   Length 5.25"

IDENTIFICATION: Adult male

 Essential Clues

+ *Black breast and belly*
+ *Black bill*
+ *Very large hummingbird*

One of our two largest hummingbirds, male Magnificent often appears almost all black, iridescence only rarely showing to full extent. Body is slender and elongated and bill is very long and straight. It has a big-headed look, and crest feathers are often raised. It appears noticeably larger when side by side with other species (except Blue-throated). Forehead and crown are iridescent purple and throat bright green. Breast and upper belly are black; lower belly is dusky. There is a small white spot behind eye. **In flight:** Tail is all dark with no white spots and only occasionally fanned.

Magnificent Male

ID Tips Note this bird's very dark overall appearance. It also appears long-bodied and long-billed. White spot behind eye is prominent.

Magnificent Hummingbird

Magnificent Male

ID Tips In this view, we see a hint of purple iridescence on top of head. Note also blue-green throat, black breast and belly, and iridescent green flanks.

Magnificent Male

ID Tips Here we see brilliant blue-green throat iridescence as well as unique black breast and belly.

Magnificent Male

ID Tips Note blue-green iridescence on throat; top of head looks dark. In this view, upper flanks show green iridescence.

IDENTIFICATION: Adult female and immature

Essential Clues

+ *Very large hummingbird*
+ *Jagged white line behind eye*
+ *Narrow white tips to outer tail feathers*
+ *Tail, rump, and back iridescent green*

This and Blue-throated Hummingbird are our largest hummingbirds, noticeably larger than other species. Female Magnificent has jagged white line behind eye. Underparts are gray, heavily spotted with darker gray and / or green. Tail, rump, and back are iridescent green, and corners of tail are narrowly tipped with white. When bird is flying, tail is only occasionally spread.

In immature males, spots of adult plumage may be seen, such as black on breast, turquoise on throat, and violet on forehead.

Voice — Call a high "dzzip." During chases, gives a skittering series of chips, "kip, kidip, kidip, kip, kidip." Has rising inflection toward end. Song, given by male, is low-pitched jumble of scratchy notes audible only at close range.

Magnificent Female

ID Tips Note irregular white line behind eye and very long bill. Rump and upper tail are iridescent green; underparts are pale and spotted with gray.

Magnificent Female

ID Tips On this bird, note eyeline, green rump, and pale underparts scaled with gray. Tail shows small white corners.

Magnificent Immature Male

ID Tips Note overall scaly appearance of underparts. This bird also shows an irregular white eyeline, very long bill, and small white tail corners.

LIFE HISTORY

Breeding

Breeds in pine-oak forests near streams at middle to high elevations (5,000–10,000 feet), with forest edges and clearings preferred. Females begin nesting in April or early May; it is unknown whether they have more than one brood.

Clutch size: 2

Incubation period: unknown; likely 15–19 days

Nestling period: 25 or more days

Nest

Usually placed on horizontal branch of maple, sycamore, or fir at height of 10–55 feet above stream. Nest is built with feather down, mosses, and other plant fibers; it is fastened with spiderwebbing and heavily coated with lichens.

Male Displays

No flight displays known. Males sing and chase females.

Other Behavior & Information

Known as Rivoli's Hummingbird until the 1980s, this is second-largest North American hummingbird. It is little studied in our area, largely because of its nomadic habits and secretiveness of females. Flower mites travel to new flowers by stowing away in Magnificent Hummingbirds' nostrils.

Feeding

Forages over wide area, visiting many plants in feeding cycle; does not tend to defend feeding territories as other species do. Magnificent Hummingbirds seem to rely heavily on insect prey, perhaps more than on nectar. They do, however, come to hummingbird feeders. The only hummingbird that dominates Magnificent is Blue-throated.

Migration

Most of population are year-round residents in Mexico, but some Magnificent Hummingbirds are short-distance migrants that breed in extreme southwestern U.S. Routes and timing are unknown, but spring arrival begins in late March, with males coming before females. Southbound departure occurs in late September to early October; males leave first, then females, then immatures. Some birds may remain in Arizona throughout winter.

Buff-bellied Adult

ID Tips Note iridescent emerald-green throat and upper breast, extensively red-based bill, and pale buffy belly.

Buff-bellied Hummingbird
Amazilia yucatanensis   Length 4.25"

IDENTIFICATION: Adult male, adult female, and immature

 Essential Clues
+ *Red bill with dark tip*
+ *Dark green throat and breast*
+ *Buffy belly*

This hummingbird appears dark overall due to its dark green throat and breast. Belly is buffy. Bill is very long, downcurved, and red with dark tip. Uppertail coverts are bronze-green. **In flight:** Note dusky wings and rufous tail. Similar Berylline has rufous in wings.

Sexes — Male and female look similar, but female has small inconspicuous patch of whitish or whitish-edged feathers at base of lower mandible.

Immatures — Throat and breast are buffy or buffy mixed with gray or green. Red on bill may be limited in extent, with more dark at tip.

Voice — Call a high-pitched "tik," usually strung together in short series. During chases gives buzzy or shrill "zeet-zeet."

Buff-bellied Adult

ID Tips Note bright rufous tail with purplish tip. Green throat, pale buffy belly, and red bill base are all visible as well.

Buff-bellied Adult

ID Tips This bird's entirely green head gives it a hooded appearance. We see mostly-red bill, buffy belly, and rufous tail as well.

Buff-bellied Adult

ID Tips Note this bird's greenish-buff rump and upper tail. Wings are dusky.

LIFE HISTORY

Breeding

Buff-bellied Hummingbirds breed in a variety of habitats, from dry scrub to woodlands. Females begin nesting in April; it is not known if they have a second brood.

Clutch size: 2

Incubation period: unknown

Nestling period: unknown

Nest

Usually placed in bush or small tree, in fork of horizontal branch 3–10 feet high. Nest is constructed with spiderwebs and other fibers, and coated with flower petals, bark, and lichens. It is not known if females reuse nests.

Buff-bellied Female

ID Tips Perched on nest with small nestlings inside. Lichens have been used to coat exterior of nest.

Male Displays

No displays have been recorded.

Other Behavior & Information

This is least-studied species of North American hummingbird; very little is known about breeding behavior or nesting. Individuals are generally seen alone.

Feeding

Buff-bellied Hummingbirds feed on wider variety of flowers than many other species, showing no strong preference for particular shape or color. They also take insects from air and foliage. Buff-bellieds chase Ruby-throated and Black-chinned Hummingbirds away from feeders; they also chase one another, apparently preferring to feed alone.

Migration

Information is scarce. Buff-bellied Hummingbirds that breed in U.S. probably migrate short distances between southern Texas and eastern Mexico. A small number even head northeast after breeding season, spending winter in southern Louisiana and Alabama. In Texas, dates of occurrence are between March and August, except around Brownsville, where species is year-round resident.

Berylline Hummingbird
Amazilia beryllina   Length 4.25"

IDENTIFICATION: Adult male, adult female, and immature

 Essential Clues

+ *Dark green throat and breast*
+ *Dark grayish-brown belly*
+ *Rufous in wings*
+ *Red on lower mandible (may not be visible)*

This hummingbird appears dark overall because of its dark green throat and breast and dark grayish-brown belly. Bill is medium length, slightly downcurved, and orange to red only on lower mandible; upper mandible is dark, as is whole tip. Uppertail coverts are dark purple. **In flight:** Note rufous wings and tail.

Berylline Adult

ID Tips Note iridescent purplish rump and upper tail. A bit of rufous coloration is visible on wing.

Berylline Male

ID Tips Note brilliant emerald-green throat and breast. Red-based lower mandible is visible, as is rufous coloration in wings.

Sexes — Similar, but female has small inconspicuous area of whitish-edged feathers at base of bill.

Voice — Call a grating trill, "dddddddt." During chases, gives high-pitched "sssst." Song is lilting series of squeaky notes with emphasis on alternate syllables and beginning with an introductory scraping note, "krrt seeBIT, seeBIT, seeBIT."

Berylline Adult

ID Tips — Note buffy edges to rump feathers. In this view, bill appears entirely black, since lower mandible cannot be seen.

Berylline Immature

ID Tips Mottled green-and-gray throat and breast; red-based lower mandible. Belly appears grayish buff.

LIFE HISTORY

Breeding

Breeds in pine-oak forests and wooded canyons at fairly high elevations (above 5,000 feet); the few U.S. breeding records are all from Arizona. Females begin nesting in June or July in Arizona and have only one brood.

Clutch size: 2

Incubation period: not known

Nestling period: about 18–20 days

Nest

In Arizona, female Berylline Hummingbirds seem to favor sycamores, in which they place nest on horizontal branch 17–25 feet high. Nest is constructed mainly of plant fibers bound with spiderwebbing and coated with lichens. Usually there are a few strands of grass trailing from bottom.

Male Displays

None known.

Other Behavior & Information

Due to lack of study, very little is known about Berylline Hummingbird's breeding or social behavior.

Feeding

Forages on a variety of flowers and defends feeding territories. Comes to feeders and probably flycatches for insects as other hummingbirds do. It is not known whether Berylline Hummingbird is dominant or subordinate in comparison to other species.

Migration

Most of population are year-round residents in Mexico. However, a few are present each summer just north of border in Arizona and New Mexico. These arrive as early as April and depart by mid-August.

Violet-crowned Hummingbird

Amazilia violiceps   Length 4.5"

IDENTIFICATION: Adult male, adult female, and immature

 Essential Clues

+ *Pure white below*
+ *Violet crown*

A large and slender hummingbird with a long, thick, slightly downcurved bill. Sexes are alike. Unique among North American hummers in having underparts almost pure white, with some brownish smudging on flanks. Upperparts plain brownish bronze except for crown and forehead, which are iridescent violet. Throat entirely plain white. Adult's bill bright red with black tip. Immatures resemble adults but lack iridescence on crown, and red color is confined to base of bill.

Voice — Call a low-pitched unmusical "ket." During chases, gives series of squeaky chips. Song is high-pitched series of down-slurred notes.

Violet-crowned Adult

ID Tips Note dull olive-brown upperparts, clean white throat and breast, black-tipped red bill, and hint of violet iridescence on crown.

Violet-crowned Adult

ID Tips Note unique pure white underparts, as well as violet crown and red bill.

Violet-crowned Adult

ID Tips This view shows violet iridescence on head. Rest of upperparts are entirely olive-brown. Pure white throat and bright red bill are distinctive.

Violet-crowned Immature

ID Tips Note scaly upperparts and mere hint of violet iridescence on crown. Underparts are rather dingy, and bill shows red on lower mandible.

129

LIFE HISTORY

Breeding

Nests in groves of sycamores and cottonwoods along streams at lower elevations of canyons. In U.S., females begin nesting in June and usually have second brood.

Clutch size: 2

Incubation period: unknown; probably 14–20 days

Nestling period: unknown; probably 3–4 weeks

Nest

Little information is available, but nest is usually placed 10–40 feet above ground in sycamore tree, at or near tip of branch. Nest is made of spiderwebs and white cottony material from trees, and adorned with lichens and twigs.

Male Displays

Unknown.

Violet-crowned

ID Tips Two nestlings sitting in nest, which is coated with lichens.

Other Behavior & Information

First recorded nesting by Violet-crowned Hummingbirds in U.S. was in 1959. They are now uncommon nesters annually in extreme southeastern Arizona and southwestern New Mexico. Information on species is scarce due to lack of field research.

Feeding

Feeding habits are not well-known, but Violet-crowned is like other hummingbirds in food choice. It frequently feeds on insects by flycatching. Perhaps due to comparatively large size, Violet-crowned Hummingbird seems to be dominant over most other hummingbirds, with possible exception of larger Blue-throated and Magnificent.

Migration

Violet-crowned Hummingbirds in U.S. are short-distance migrants from western Mexico. Details of migration are unknown, but spring arrival on U.S. breeding grounds is in early May. By end of September, most Violet-crowneds have moved south. It is assumed that, as with other humming-birds, males migrate first, followed by females and, in fall, immatures. Vagrants (which are rare) have occurred in southern California and western Texas. A scattering of individuals may spend winter in southern Arizona.

Broad-billed Hummingbird
Cynanthus latirostris   Length 4.0"

IDENTIFICATION: Adult male

 Essential Clues

+ *Red bill tipped with black*
+ *Dark green breast and belly (throat and crown blue)*
+ *No white ear stripe (just small white spot behind eye)*

A slender-bodied hummingbird with gradually sloping forehead and long downcurved bill. Male is very dark with bright red bill tipped with black. Throat and forehead are iridescent blue; rest of body is dark green, except for white undertail coverts. There is a small white spot behind eye. **In flight:** Broad and noticeably forked tail has glossy blue feathers narrowly tipped with gray.

Broad-billed Male

ID Tips Note this bird's long red-based bill, blue throat, and notched blue tail. Breast and upper belly appear dark in this view.

Broad-billed Hummingbird

Broad-billed Male

ID Tips Note red-based bill, blue throat, and green breast and belly. There is a small white spot behind eye. In shape, this bird appears rather long and slender.

Broad-billed Male

ID Tips This view shows brilliant iridescent blue throat and green breast and belly. Undertail coverts are whitish.

IDENTIFICATION: Adult female and immature

Essential Clues

+ *Thin whitish line over and behind eye*
+ *Gray ear patch and forehead*
+ *Small*
+ *Red at base of lower mandible (sometimes inconspicuous)*

A slender-bodied hummingbird with long slightly downcurved bill. It has a flat low forehead. It is light gray from throat to belly. A thin whitish stripe extends back from over eye. Lower mandible is red at base. There is a gray ear patch. Back feathers are iridescent green with lighter edges.

Immature male has patches of blue iridescence on throat and flecks of green on body.

Voice — Main call is two-syllable static crackle, "chi-chit." Also gives a high "zeet." Chase call is rapid series of chips that run together at the end. Song, given by male, is high-pitched string of tinkling notes following introductory chip.

Broad-billed Female

ID Tips Note characteristic whitish eyeline, gray forehead and ear patch, and red base of lower mandible. Throat, breast, and belly are pale gray.

Broad-billed Female

ID Tips: Here we see white eyeline, red lower mandible, and gray underparts. Note green flanks and grayish tip of bluish tail.

Broad-billed Immature Male

ID Tips: Beginning to acquire blue iridescence on throat and green on breast. Crown feathers have buff edges, and base of bill is reddish.

LIFE HISTORY

Breeding

Broad-billed Hummingbirds breed in remote dry canyons at elevations below 6,000 feet. Females begin nesting in mid-April and usually begin a second brood in early July.

Clutch size: 2

Incubation period: probably 15–19 days

Nestling period: about 20–26 days

Nest

Usually placed within 6 feet of ground and close to rocky outcroppings. Nest is built so as to resemble a ball of detritus — bark, grass, and leaves — that can catch on branches during floods. Occasionally, lichens are used to coat outside of nest. Females may reuse nests or build new nest on top of old one.

Male Displays

Pendulum display — Male does a pendulum display usually as courtship but also as aggression. When displaying to female, he first hovers within inches of her. He then flies side to side in a series of arcs while his wings create a piercing

Broad-billed Female

ID Tips On nest incubating. Note nest's jumbled untidy appearance.

buzz and he chatters constantly. After displaying, male either flies to perch close at hand or chases female. Males may also perform pendulum display in order to drive other males out of a territory.

Other Behavior & Information

Broad-billed Hummingbirds may join in gatherings of birds that "mob" Ferruginous Pygmy-Owls, American Kestrels, and Rough-winged Swallows. Not much is known about this species' social life or breeding behavior, and nesting information is also lacking.

Feeding

Forages over wide area, visiting many plants in feeding cycle; does not defend feeding territories as other species do, instead uses very large home range. Like other hummingbirds, flycatches for insects and takes them from plants. Broad-billed Hummingbirds are not particularly aggressive; they rarely chase other hummingbirds besides one another.

Migration

Most of the population are year-round residents in western Mexico, but some Broad-billed Hummingbirds are short-distance migrants that breed in U.S. Migration route is unknown, but males arrive on U.S. breeding grounds in mid-March, followed by females soon after. Adult males move south in late August; females and young begin to migrate in about mid-September. In Big Bend area of Texas, however, where they are rare, their migration schedule is a month later. The Broad-billed Hummingbird is fairly widespread as a vagrant, having occurred in Oregon, California, central Arizona and New Mexico, Texas, Nevada, Utah, Louisiana, Mississippi, and South Carolina.

Blue-throated Hummingbird
Lampornis clemenciae   Length 5.0″

IDENTIFICATION: Adult male

 Essential Clues

+ *Large hummingbird*
+ *Blue throat*
+ *Dark gray breast and belly*

This and the Magnificent Hummingbird are our largest hummingbirds, noticeably larger than other species. A large hummingbird with relatively short straight bill. Fairly dark overall with distinctive cobalt-blue iridescence on throat and dark gray on rest of underparts. Face has two thin white lines, one behind eye and other a "mustache" off base of bill. Rump is bronze. **In flight:** Very large tail is both long and broad and often fanned, showing extensive white tips on corners. The Blue-throated has slower wingbeats than our other hummingbirds.

Blue-throated Male

ID Tips White eyeline and mustache, blue iridescence on throat, and short straight bill. Rump is bronze-copper, and upper tail is bluish black.

Blue-throated Male

ID Tips Large white tail corners are unique among adult male hummingbirds. Note gray underparts, white face stripes, and short straight bill.

Blue-throated Male

ID Tips Distinctive brilliant cobalt-blue throat. Also easily seen are dark gray underparts and large white tail corners.

IDENTIFICATION: Adult female and immature

Essential Clues

+ *Large hummingbird*
+ *Long even white line behind eye*
+ *Broad white tips to outer tail feathers*
+ *Blackish tail contrasts with lighter bronze rump*

This and the Magnificent Hummingbird are our largest hummingbirds, noticeably larger than other species. The Blue-throated has long thin white stripe behind eye. Throat and underparts are plain gray. Pale bronze lower back and rump contrast with darker tail, which is black with bluish tinge. Broad white tips to outer tail feathers are often seen as bird spreads tail in flight.

Voice — Call a piercing "tsit," often very frequent. During chases, gives an abrupt "kidit, sit," with third note similar to typical call note. Song is audible only at close range, consisting of rattles and sibilant whistles, variable in length and quality. The Blue-throated Hummingbird's song is unusually complex and sung by adults of both sexes.

Blue-throated Female

ID Tips Note white stripe behind eye and faint white "mustache" extending back from all-black bill. Throat, breast, and belly are entirely gray.

Blue-throated Female

ID Tips This bird shows even white stripe behind eye, bronze rump, and glossy bluish-black upper tail.

Blue-throated Female

ID Tips Note white eyestripe and mustache, and pale gray underparts. Also, bronze rump and bluish-black upper tail.

LIFE HISTORY

Breeding

Blue-throated Hummingbirds are quite choosy about their breeding habitat, insisting on wooded areas by mountain streams. Females nest from mid-April through September, usually having 2 broods and sometimes 3.

Clutch size: 2; rarely 1

Incubation period: 17–19 days

Nestling period: 24–26 days

Nest

Nest can be built in a variety of situations, but female prefers an overhang above nest site, such as rock ledge or cave opening. She also often nests on human-made structures, such as an outdoor lamp. Nest is attached to exposed roots, hanging branches, wires, chains, or hooks. Outside is coated with

Blue-throated Female

ID Tips On nest incubating. Nest is anchored to light with spiderwebbing.

mosses when available, and if not, nest is not camouflaged. Females may take material from old nests to use in building new ones. They also sometimes nest in abandoned Black Phoebe nests.

Male Displays

Males apparently do not perform flight displays, but they chase females during mating season.

Other Behavior & Information

Females fiercely defend nestlings; some have attacked Mountain Spiny Lizards and Canyon Wrens and driven them into hiding.

Feeding

Eats flower nectar and goes to hummingbird feeders. Gleans insects from vegetation, hovering and plucking from bark and foliage; also raids spiderwebs. The Blue-throated Hummingbird is at top of hummingbird hierarchy at feeders and natural sources of nectar. Extremely aggressive during breeding, males frequently chase other hummingbirds and stab at them with bill. Males also chase birds of other

species, including Pine Siskins, which are not a threat to hummingbirds.

Migration

Blue-throated Hummingbirds are short-distance migrants; exact routes they take are unknown. Breeding and winter ranges are expanding northward. Spring migrants begin to return to breeding grounds in mid-March. In September, adult males head south, followed later by females and immatures. There have been fall sightings in Utah, Colorado, Texas, Louisiana, and Alabama. In addition, a few individuals now winter in Arizona.

Easy Key to Hummingbird Identification

HUMMINGBIRDS WITH DARK THROATS

Dark throat and dark upper breast: Go to page 30.

Buff-bellied, White-eared, Broad-billed, Berylline

Blue-throated, Magnificent

Dark throat and whitish upper breast: Go to page 32.

Allen's, Rufous

Calliope, Costa's, Lucifer

Ruby-throated, Anna's, Black-chinned, Broad-tailed

HUMMINGBIRDS WITH MOSTLY LIGHT THROATS

Conspicuous white eyeline:
Go to page 38.

Broad-billed, White-eared

Magnificent, Blue-throated

Buffy flanks: Go to page 40.

Lucifer

Rufous, Allen's

Broad-tailed, Calliope

White or green flanks and no eyeline:
Go to page 42.

Violet-crowned

Anna's, Costa's

Black-chinned, Ruby-throated